Clas
F

A Load of New Nonsense

Also available:

Tales from an Alien's Toe

ISBN 978-0-9559975-1-8

written by Mike Lucas and published by Ginger Cat Publishing.

A Load of New Nonsense

Mike Lucas

A Ginger Cat Book

Based on the original scribblings of an alien
Stolen and adapted by Mike Lucas
Text Copyright © 2008 Mike Lucas
Cover illustration by James Robinson

First edition 2008
First published on Earth (in particular Great Britain) 2008 by
Ginger Cat Publishing

All rights reserved. No part of this publication may be reproduced, stored in a retrieval system, or transmitted in any form or by any means, electronic, mechanical, photocopy, recording or otherwise, without prior written permission of the copyright owner. Nor can it be circulated in any form of binding or cover other than that in which it is published and without similar condition including this condition being imposed on a subsequent purchaser.

ISBN 978-0-9559975-0-1

www.gingercatpublishing.co.uk

Acknowledgement

*I'd like to thank someone who's helped me realise my dream.
He's staring back at me right now from my computer screen.
Without his dedication to the book you see today,
It would never have been possible to say what I now say.*

Thank you.

**Dedicated to Hope and Christian -
My honest critics**

**Written for children everywhere.
May you be good to the world
And may the world be good to you.**

Contents

'Silly' Poems   5

Monsters in my car	7
Purple-leaved orange disease	11
The cow who didn't want to be in a poem	12
A little light work	16
Why animals don't have computers	17
The invention that could have saved the dinosaurs	19
Sir Tortoise and the wheelbarrow	20
Onions	23
Poemski	24
Orang-utan at the cinema	27
A sad story	28
Mad duck	29
Scared in the woods	30
My granny's banana	31
A monster's Hallowe'en	32
Philoneas Fluff	33
A prehistoric visitor	36
Quing-quong pie	37
That field has got a crease in it	40
Tasty guests	41

'Animal' Poems   43

Limpets	45
The aardvark and the zebra	46
Worms are ~~not~~ funny	47
The rarest of animals	48
A horse in a car	49
The little penguin	50
The whale's teeth	52
Wannabe wildebeest	54

Don't get down	55
Harry and the Hoover	56
Wannabe wallaby	57
A wild birthday	58
Beetle juice	61
The monkey in my class	62
Get out of the mud	63
A fine balance	64
A small amphibian	68
Not an otter	69
Crazy hedgehog	70
Judge Gerbil and the rat	71
'Young' Poems	**73**
Down in the woods where the bears go, "Boo!"	75
Countdown	76
My wish for vegetables	77
What makes the waves?	78
Smelly toes	79
A strange tribe	80
Dizzy below	81
Where to go today?	82
Pick a favourite	83
I'm not tired	84
What's the sense of weather?	85
How high is the sky?	86
My penny	87
Little Johnny (a cautionary tale for children)	88
Big eared baldy baby	91
Do you know where the Bobblebears go?	92
Little boy, fluffy toy	94
The rocking horse	95
My fateful wish	96
Mum! Mum! Mum!	97

'Language' Poems   99

No poems are coming tonight   101
Gobbledegook   102
Breaking the rule   103
The colour of my poem   104
Useless poem   105
How (not) to write a limerick   106
Writer's block   107
M.N.E.M.O.N.I.C.   108
The motivation behind a poem   109
A body of grammar   110
A very different poem   111
The same as opposite   112
Somefink   113
Eether or neether?   114
Granama   115
Hoity-toity poem   116

'My' Poems   117

My hair   119
My family (when I'm away)   120
My gran   121
My cats (when they lived in Switzerland)   122
My bogey box   123
My hamster   124
My cat, Max   125
My Christmas birthday   126
My Great Uncle Tommy   127
My disgusting habit   128
My visitor   129
My bath   132
My little toe   133
My broken radio   134
My luvvy duvvy poem   135
My epitaph   136

Mike Lucas

'Silly' Poems

These poems are called 'Silly',
But they might just be obscure.
It doesn't mean they're nonsense, but they could be.
They're written willy-nilly
And the rhyming is quite pure.
But if you find sometimes it isn't, then it should be.

Mike Lucas

Monsters in my car

I was driving home from work one day,
The weather had turned cold.
A monster and his family
Went and jumped into the road.

Their seven heads (one hadn't yet grown)
Looked up and down the car.
And the father (at least I think it was)
Asked, "Are you going far?"

Now, what to say on that cold day
To monsters in the road,
With fifteen arms (I'd lost my count)
And skin as gold as…well, gold?

"I'm going home to my warm house -
It's only small," I said.
The mother monster (she had long hair)
Said, "We only want a bed."

So in they climbed, the four of them -
Their nineteen legs were squashed.
I left a window open
Because I don't believe they'd washed.

We drove through snow, they never spoke,
Except to ask my name.
And to say that they were Schmoogles
And from whereabouts they came.

And they asked me if I knew at all
Of the spotted Ignaroo.
I thought about it for a while
And said, "I don't believe I do."

They said that was a shame because,
The night being so cold…
And then another monster
Went and jumped into the road.

"The Ignaroo!" my monsters cried
(I was quite attached by then).
I stopped the car and, of the
Ignaroo, I counted ten.

My house was small, oh that was true,
But my car was smaller still.
But the Ignaroo just clambered in
And we lumbered up the hill.

We all shook hands, my monsters,
The Ignaroo and me.
And then a tiny monster asked,
"Excuse me, what's for tea?"

"I hadn't thought of that," I said,
But then I passed a sign
Which read *'Monster Supermarket Sale'*,
So I thought that would do fine.

Have you ever shopped for monsters?
It's no fun with wonky wheels.
But seven trolleys later
I had fourteen monster meals.

Returning to the car
With monsters squished and squashed inside,
Mmm...where to put the shopping
Whilst continuing the ride?

There was just one small place empty
And, my arms weighed down with fruit,
I opened up the rear
To find twelve monsters in the boot.

"Hello, we are the Grinsters.
Nice to meet you. How d'you do?
The Schmoogles and the Ignaroo
Said we were welcome too."

I closed the boot – well, what to do?
Where would all of this stop?
And, opening up the driver's door,
I said, "You all have to move up!"

And they all did. The monsters
Really are a bendy race.
There were knees and elbows and other bits
Crammed into every face.

The trolleys finally emptied,
I squeezed into my car,
And started on my way again.
"It isn't very far."

Ten minutes later we arrived.
I stopped the engine there,
And asked the monsters to get out,
Then climbed out of my chair.

And so the monsters followed me,
Schmoogles and Ignaroo,
Exploding from my little car,
Each carrying some food.

"Don't forget the Grinsters,"
A little monster said.
And then the boot flew open
And bonked me on the head.

When I awoke the house was quiet,
No monster was in sight.
It must have been a dream, I thought
As I turned out the light.

I climbed the stairs and brushed my teeth.
How good to be at home,
With the snow and wind so wild outside,
How nice to be alone.

I climbed in bed, and felt some fur.
But I didn't have a pet.
And suddenly…twenty six loud voices cried…
"IS BREAKFAST READY YET?!"

Purple-leaved orange disease

I once met an orange with purpley leaves,
Who cycled beside me and asked if I'd please
Spare a penny for purple-leaved orange disease.
I looked in my pocket for a penny donation,
But all that I found was a button with lace on.
"A button is fine," said that fruit from the Cape,
And then cycled off with an orange-leaved grape.

The cow who didn't want to be in a poem

The cow walked through the outback
(Don't ask me why he's there).
He ate some grass
And moo-ed on past,
A cow without a care.
When he came upon a kangaroo
Jumping up and down.
I'll have a bit of that, he thought,
And turned him upside down.

I came across the kangaroo
Sitting by a tree.
His paws were in his pocket
And his head between his knees.
I asked him what had happened
And he told me of his woes.
A cow had pushed him over
And had left him with bare toes.
"If I see that rotten cow," he said,
"I'll give him such a thump.
'Cause when he stole my favourite shoes
He also stole my jump."

The cow jumped down the river
(Don't ask me, I'm not sure).
He chewed a bit
And moo'ed a bit,
And chewed a bit some more.
When he came upon a crocodile
Snapping on some chips.
I'll have a bit of that, he thought,
And kissed him on the lips.

I came across the crocodile
Lying by a lake.
His tail was in the water
And he was sucking on some cake.
I asked him what had happened
And he moaned a sorry moan.
"He kissed my teeth out of my mouth
And stuck them in his own.
If I see that rotten cow," he said,
"I'll give him such a slap.
'Cause when he stole my chopping chops
He also stole my snap."

The snappy cow jumped through the jungle
(I told you, I don't know).
He snapped at trees,
And cheddar cheese
He'd brought with him from home.
When he came upon a tiger
Slinking through the trees.
I'll have a bit of that, he thought,
And gave the cat a squeeze.

I came across the tiger
Stretched out on a rock.
He looked at me and blushed a bit
(He wore a purple frock).
I asked him what had happened
And from his eye a big tear rolled.
He said, "That cow gave me a hug
And left me feeling cold.
If I see that rotten cow," he said,
"I'll give him such a swipe.
'Cause when he stole my nice warm fur
He also stole my stripe."

The stripy, snappy, jumpy cow
(I'd tell you if I knew)
Had had enough
Of all this stuff
And jumped into the zoo.
When he came upon a creature,
The strangest creature in the land.
I'll have a bit of that, he thought,
And took him by the hand.

I came across the cow that day
Whilst visiting the zoo.
I was trying to end a poem
Before I sent it off to you.
There's something odd about that cow,
I thought aloud, and then
That snappy, stripy animal
Jumped up and took my pen.
If I catch that rotten cow, I thought,
I'll feed him to the birds.
'Cause when he stole my fountain pen
He also stole my words.

I am a jumpy, snappy, stripy cow,
But I never asked to be.
I chewed on grass,
The days went past,
I moo'ed contentedly,
When a poet with no business
Picked up a pen and said,
I'll make that cow catch a kangaroo
And tip him on his head.
Then make him kiss a crocodile.
I didn't have a say.

And cuddle with a tiger
In a most embarrassing way.

So I met with him this morning
And I took away his pen.
He won't be writing nonsense
Or ridiculing me again.
I took him round the zoo you see,
To every cage, took him with me.
And whilst he shouted, "Let me out!"
'Twas him I wrote about.

A little light work

I planted a bulb in the soil in September
And left it alone for the day.
I sat in the dark till I finally remembered
And went out to check it in May.

The plant that had sprouted was shiny and flash,
But there wasn't a flower in sight.
So I dug up the bulb and I took it inside
And I plugged it back into the light.

Why animals don't have computers

They bought a computer,
Took it home on a scooter,
The Mouse and the Kangaroo.

They unpacked the box,
Then they called wise old Fox
To clarify what they should do.

It all fitted nicely,
And connected precisely,
Just like the instructions required.

And before Alligator
Dropped round for potat'er
Nearly all of the system was wired.

"Now there's just one thing left,
But I think we're bereft
Of this item - I can't see it here."

So they all looked around
(Some looked up, some looked down),
Till the Kangaroo had an idea.

He jumped up off the floor,
Pointed straight out the door,
Shouted, "Look at that pig in a rocket!"

Whilst they fell for the joke,
The Mouse went up in smoke,
As he'd plugged its tail into the socket.

Well, the animals toasted,
As their smallest friend roasted,
And opened a bottle of bubbly.

Now the Mouse was connected,
And virus protected.
They were finally online. Lubbly-Jubbly.

The invention that could have saved the dinosaurs

The dinosaurs wouldn't have gotten extinct
If they'd only invented the pocket.
They'd have had a good place to put all of their tools,
And then used them for building a rocket.

Sir Tortoise and the wheelbarrow

Sir Tortoise the old anthropologist
Was always concerned there was something he'd missed.
He'd been to the East and he'd been to the West.
His feet were worn down and his shell was a mess.
He'd done everything that could ever be done,
But he felt he was missing just one.

So he called to his partner, the brilliant Lord Sparrow,
As tough as they come and as straight as an arrow.
He said, "Look, old Sparrow, I've been lots of places,
Discovered new lands and uncovered new races.
There isn't a corner that I haven't seen,
Or a place where Sir Tortoise ain't been."

The old bird looked down and he thought for a bit.
Sir T. was well travelled, he had to admit.
He'd fulfilled his ambitions, overcome all his fears,
But Lord S. was the one who'd had all the ideas.
"Circumnavigation is the key," said Lord Sparrow,
"But performed in a garden wheelbarrow."

"Why, that's it!" said Sir T, "by me shell you are right.
I'll pack straight away and get started tonight."
So he filled up his shell with his gear for survival.
He acted in haste, for he had him a rival.
"I will not let that dratted McFrog steal my thunder
From that rock that he likes to hide under!"

But McFrog had been watching the two of them talk,
And he'd heard everything, every grunt, squeak and squawk.
Then he hopped up and down as he hatched out his plan.
"If Sir Tortoise can do it, then McFrog surely can.

I'll be drinking my bubbly when he crosses the line.
That garden wheelbarrow is mine."

Lord Sparrow expected McFrog to appear.
So, as was his duty, he hatched an idea.
And whilst old Sir Tortoise prepared for his trip,
He watched as McFrog did a hop, jump and skip.
He vowed that the Frog would be sent to the gallows
For stealing the garden wheelbarrow.

So McFrog climbed aboard and prepared for the ride,
And he heard, as he did, a bird's soft lullaby.
Just forty winks, it'll do me no harm.
And just to be sure, let me set my alarm.
And then, closing his eyes, old McFrog fell asleep,
And never again made a peep.

The gardener lay dreaming the nicest of dreams,
Of tractors and cornfields, of strawberries and cream,
When he heard at his window a bird, *tap! tap! tap!*
So he tossed and he turned till he woke from his nap.
"That damn sparrow's a nuisance," the gardener did mumble,
And out of his bed he did stumble.

The gardener got dressed and went down the stairs yawning.
He wasn't too bright and he thought it was morning.
He ached from hard labour the previous day,
From spreading the muck and from moving the hay.
But he swallowed some pills as a temporary cure,
And then went out to move more manure.

Whilst Sir Tortoise lay resting before his long trip,
In the barrow McFrog was enjoying his kip.
Lord Sparrow returned to his branch with a smirk.

He'd fooled the old gardener from bed to his work.
The old man set out, unaware of the joke.
And McFrog would soon silently croak.

There was a tonne and a half of the steaming old muck,
More than enough poo to fill a small truck.
But it had to be moved with just blood, sweat and tears.
He'd been doing this job for near forty five years.
So he picked up his tools, and he trudged past the sallow,
And then lifted the garden wheelbarrow.

Lord Sparrow looked on from his nest way up high,
And the old gardener worked till his old throat was dry.
He parted the poo like a modern day Moses,
Then walked his old barrow towards the Duke's roses,
And made a new pile that smelled rancid and rotten,
With McFrog lying dead at the bottom.

The gardener was finished, the sun on the rise,
The wheelbarrow back and surrounded by flies,
When Sir Tortoise arose from his long evening rest
And boarded the barrow for his trip to the West.
With his shell neatly packed with his gear for survival,
Surprised with the absence of McFrog, his old rival,
He looked up at Lord Sparrow asleep in the tree
And said, "Where would you be without me?"

Onions

I went to buy an onion from the grocer in the town.
He explained all of the different types and so I wrote them down.
I decided that I liked the green ones better than the red.
He put them in a paper bag and, "That's shallot," he said.

Poemski

Old Man Polatski,
He lived in a flatski
And kept a black catski
And called him Big Fred.

Old Miss Kolowski,
She lived in a houseki,
Discovered a mouseki
And wanted it dead.

Said Old Miss Kolowski
To Old Man Polatski,
"Can you send your catski
To kill mouseki dead?"

Said Old Man Polatski
To Old Miss Kolowski,
"Big Fred will catch mouseki
And will be well fed."

He picked up his catski,
Enjoying his napski
And said to him, "Catchski
A ratski, Big Fred!"

Polatski's pet catski
Walked slow to the houseki
And found the poor mouseki
Asleep on the bed.

While Old Miss Kolowski
And Old Man Polatski
Stayed inside the flatski
Till mouseki was dead.

Catski chased mouseki
All over the houseki,
Upski and Downski
The two of them fled.

Then catski caught mouseki
(I'm not quite sure howski)
And said to it, "Mouseki,
I want us to wed."

And mouseki to catski
Said, "But how is thatski?
You live in a flatski.
Please tell me, Big Fred."

And catski to mouseki
Said, "Please listen nowski.
See, Old Miss Polowski,
She wanted your head.

She asked Old Polatski
To send this big catski
To kill a big ratski
Who lay on her bed.

But you're a smart mouseki
And it's a nice houseki,
So we should not rowski
But live here instead."

So catski and mouseki,
They lived in the houseki
Without Miss Kolowski
And soon they were wed.

Kolowski? Polatski?
They're still in the flatski.
And that, sir, is thatski,
And all is now said.

Orang-utan at the cinema

The orang-utan gave out the end of the film
At the cinema every time.
He'd sit at the back,
All alone in the black,
And await the penultimate line.

And just as the audience all held their breaths
And sat on the edge of their seats,
The orangutan stood,
And yelled loud as he could,
"I've seen this – the killer is Pete!"

All the people in front put their heads in their hands,
And then booed at that ginger gorilla.
How dare he hide there,
With his feet in the air,
And ruin the end of the thriller.

In cinemas here and in cinemas there
The public stood up to complain.
Now you'll no longer find
That old ape sat behind,
And the twist at the end will remain.

A sad story

Tigger had a sneeze and cough.
He couldn't shake the symptoms off.
His eyes would water, nose would run.
He wasn't having fun.

Tigger went to see the vet.
She said, "These symptoms that you get.
Tell me, when do they occur?"
Tigger didn't purr.

"Do they appear inside the house?
Before you eat or after mouse?
In the litter, when you drink?"
Tigger had a think.

"I start to cough each morning time,
When she comes in at half past nine.
It lasts until the night," he said,
"When she goes off to bed."

"Just as I thought, bad news I fear.
Though I'm aware you hold her dear,
Your cough appears when she's around.
She has to be put down."

It's over now, Tigger supposes.
He buried her beneath the roses.
His allergy to humans gone,
Tigger's moving on.

Mad duck

"Moo," said the duck,
"That's just my luck,
To be struck down with mad cow disease."

"Quack," said the cow,
"I don't quite know how
That duck milk gets made into cheese."

Scared in the woods

The woods were dark,
The rain was cold.
There was no-one there but me.
I didn't know
Which way to go,
For I could hardly see.

Then something ran
Across my path.
I jumped and held my breath.
I looked and saw
A rabbit which
Had scared me half to death.

The rabbit twitched
And looked my way.
I smiled at it and then…
A monster came
And ate it up
And disappeared again.

My granny's banana

My granny had a pet banana.
She kept it in the shed.
She'd dress it in pyjamas
And she'd tuck it into bed.

And then, one day, my granny died.
She lay there all alone,
Until some neighbours found her there
Whilst ransacking her home.

The poor banana lay there too,
In his PJ's, nearly dead.
His skin was black and mottled.
There were maggots in his head.

And finally he slipped away,
To fall upon the floor.
The neighbours put him in the bin.
Banana was no more.

Now my granny is in heaven,
And she's looking down at me,
With her little yellow angel,
In pyjamas, on her knee.

A monster's Hallowe'en

"I want to dress up like a human,"
Said the monster at Hallowe'en.
"Mum, make me a suit
That makes me look cute;
A little less scary and green."

"I want to dress up like a human,
And go out to play treat or trick.
If they give me some goodies
I'll take off my hoodie
And scare them until they are sick."

Philoneas Fluff

Philoneas Fluff kept all kinds of stuff
In his house on a cliff by the sea.
He was such an old moaner, a miser and loner,
And loved not a being but he.

Now Philoneas had not the room for a mouse
Or a cricket, an ant or a flea.
He kept his house guarded and never discarded
A pencil, a pin or a pea.

His house was a hovel straight out of a novel
Of a wicked, old man all alone.
His dog was so vicious, found nowt more delicious
Than chewing on fresh human bone.

One day, whilst out playing, some children came straying
Mistakenly onto his land.
They played with a ball and a Frisbee, that's all,
And they had them a picnic all planned.

Well, Philoneas stared from his window, and glared
At the boys as they played in the sun.
And he waited intently, for he knew, evidently,
That the ball or the Frisbee would come.

He had not long to wait as the great iron gate
Could not keep out the young children's toys.
And the Frisbee flew over, to land in the clover,
And after it came the small boys.

Philoneas Fluff and his dog, Rabid Ruff,
Couldn't make with much haste through the house.
For you may well recall that along the great hall
There was not enough room for a mouse.

But P. Fluff was so lean, and his dog was so mean,
That they pushed all the rubbish aside.
Very soon they were there, that maleficent pair,
And the front door was pulled open wide.

Then the children all shrieked, and one boy even leaked,
With the fear for the man at the door.
Up till then they'd resisted the myth that existed
Of old Fluff and his beast by the shore.

"You 'orrible brats, with your things! Give me that!"
Said Philoneas Fluff to the lads.
"Gruff, ruff, ruff, huff, ruff, gruff!" said the dog of P. Fluff,
Which meant, "Me bite their bones? Let me, Dad!"

How the boys looked in horror, and one looked in sorro',
As the dog bit the Frisbee in three.
And he threw the disc strongly, and ever so longly,
Right over the cliff to the sea.

Then the two bent in laughter, the dog and his master.
Such misfortune for others was fun.
The poor boys stood sobbing because of the robbing,
Then started to turn round and run.

But the Fluff man said, "Boy, go and fetch me that toy!
Bring it back to add to our collection."
Ruff grunted and bounded. How bad that dog sounded!
And snatched the ball from their protection.

The ball, it was dropped. Then the ball, it was popped,
As the kids vaulted over the fence.
Rabid Ruff stood there panting, Philoneas ranting,
Neither man nor beast making much sense.

So there's Ruff with the ball, which looks flattened and small,
And a dastardly grinning P. Fluff.
"Come then, my dear mutt, their ball's useless now, but
We shall put it with all of our stuff."

So Philoneas Fluff went back home to his stuff
With one other small item to store.
And he squeezed the ball in through a gap thin as skin,
Till the house couldn't take any more.

With a creak and a crack from the base of the shack
Came a judder, a shudder and screech.
Then Philoneas Fluff, Rabid Ruff and their stuff
Toppled over the cliff to the beach.

How the children applauded (I believe that they all did)
And walked to the edge of the land.
And far down on the ground, with his stuff and his hound,
Lay Philoneas dead on the sand.

So if you keep stuff, and it's more than enough,
Build your house far away from the sea.
Build it well, build it strongly or, rightly or wrongly,
Your downfall it surely will be.

A prehistoric visitor

A dinosaur came and knocked on my door,
And asked to borrow some honey.
I was shocked and surprised,
But later surmised
That he'd probably run out of money.

Quing-quong pie

They landed in a field in Norwich,
Fed up with their milk on porridge,
Conversed with all the sheep
And promised that they meant no harm.

And then the chief alien invader,
From the planet Zig Zog, made a
Full transmission to the leader
Of the local mutton farm.

"Your loyal subjects will all die
If we don't get some quing-quong pie,
A unique delicacy
From our planet far away."

The local farmer heard the noise
And summoned up his wife and boys,
Who all stood round discussing
How a quing-quong pie is made.

"We will give you fifteen minutes
To discover what is in it.
Then I start evaporating
Your pathetic little beasts.

My faithful army has flown far,
From up there on that shining star,
And not one will move a muscle
Till on quing-quong pie they feast."

The farmer walked up to the chief
And offered him a pie of beef,
Or chicken, pork or lamb
(At that, the sheep all moved aside).

But the chief just stood there stubborn
(My gosh, how his feet were rubbing).
He just wanted to sit down
And get some quing-quong pie inside.

The old farmer stood there blankly.
He was simply flummoxed, frankly.
Then the chief turned round and pointed
At his army in their ship.

With green faces at the port-holes,
They all looked so hungry, poor souls.
How their rumbling tummies wished
They'd packed some quing-quong for the trip.

"If you cannot give us pie
Then you must be prepared to die,"
Said the chief invader, pointing
Something strange at everyone.

Then the farmer's wife went, "Aaaah!"
And a sheep nearby went, "Baaa."
As the chief tightened his tentacle
Upon his laser gun.

But on stepping up to shoot
He heard a noise beneath his boot
And, looking down, he found a substance
That was squishy, brown and dry.

Then the chief bent down and picked it.
Then he smelled it, then he licked it.
To his army, he looked up and shouted,
"Behold, quing-quong pie!"

So the farmer's loving wife
Was asked to go and fetch a knife,
And they cut it into slices
For the army all to share.

Then the chief alien invader
Shook the farmer's hand and made a
Speech of thanks and took his army,
And then flew into the air.

Now, every now and then near Norwich,
Disenchanted with their porridge,
Come the aliens from galaxies
Up in the distant sky.

And the farmer's sheep get working
(Whilst the farmer's slyly smirking),
Munching grass to make the universe's
Perfect quing-quong pie.

That field has got a crease in it

That field has got a crease in it -
The sheep have fallen over.
They've landed in a woolly puddle
Amongst the grass and clover.

Their legs are sticking upwards
And their feet are in the air.
They're all crying their eyes out
Because there's nobody that cares.

But here comes the old farmer.
The sheep can all stop crying.
He's got a trailer on the back
With a gigantic iron.

He pulls the sheep out of the crease
And irons out the field.
Then looks at that big woolly pile,
All soggy and congealed.

He strings a string from tree to tree.
The sheep all baa and cry.
He picks the sheep up one by one.
He needs to get them dry.

The sheep are all quite happy now.
There's no more sheepy tears.
The sun is out, the field is flat.
They're pegged out by the ears.

Tasty guests

There are poor, starving tribes in the Amazon jungle
Who find themselves feeling deliciously humble
When tasty explorers drop in on their village for tea.
They consider their lives unequivocally blessed
When their tasty and savoury honorary guests
Warm to their hosts, so consumed by their sweet charity.

'Animal' Poems

These poems are called 'Animal',
And each will have a beast.
They may have more than one or none at all.
I lied about the last bit,
There'll be one in there at least.
It may be big but may be very small.

Limpets

"What's the point of a limpet?"
Said a slug to a passing snail.
"I don't mean to mock,
But they suck on a rock
And can't even leave a trail.

I'd hate to be a limpet.
What a useless thing to be -
Some wobbly gel
In a raggedy shell.
They're not like you and me."

The aardvark and the zebra

The aardvark should be filled with glee
To be first in the dictionary.
And when it comes to scrabble score
It doesn't do bad (a V's worth four).
'A' power as good as the Armada,
There's no other vark that's aarder.
But for poets it's easy prey -
The aardvark cannot hide away.

The zebra should be quite upset,
The last one in the alphabet.
In scrabble sixteen is its score,
Like aardvark's is - no less, no more.
Though Z's are rare, it has just one -
The same as zero, not much fun.
But wait! A zebu has walked past.
The zebra is no longer last.

Worms are ~~not~~ funny

What's so funny about a worm,
That has no legs but has a squirm?
Is slippery, slimy, sluggish and slow?
And hasn't a knee or a foot or a toe?
What's so funny? I don't know.
But it is.

The rarest of animals

The Upside Down Bird, you may well have heard, is a very unusual
creature.
Apart from the obvious (look at its name), it has other distinguishing
features.
It feeds on small rodents that skip through the sky -
A bit of a problem as it cannot fly.
It lives only in countries that start with a Q.
For a bird that can't read that's a hard thing to do.
And what's more, that country must end in a Z.
Since the downfall of Quz,
The Upside Down Bird is now dead.

The Inside Out Hare, you may be aware, is a very peculiar mammal.
It's not very hairy, but yucky and scary, with a hump on its back like
a camel.
To mate with the female, it awaits her shrill call -
Not good as the female has no voice at all.
It lives only in packs of a hundred and one.
For a hare that can't count, that's not easily done.
And what's more, when it sees green it eats its own head.
Since it lives in the forest,
The Inside Out Hare is now dead.

The Back to Front Trout, you may have worked out, is a one of a kind
sort of fish.
With a head for a fin and a fin for a head, it has itself only one wish -
To meet with another fish just like itself -
Unlikely, as it lives in a bowl on a shelf.
It spells out its name back to front on the glass.
For a fish that can't write that's a pain in the neck.
And what's more, it must write it along the outside.
Since a fish needs its water,
The Back to Front Trout has just died.

A horse in a car

A horse in a car
Won't get very far,
But quite a lot further
Than a slug in a jar.

The little penguin

The little penguin stood up high upon the icy ledge.
He flapped his flaps, breathed in deep and moved towards the edge.
He stared down at the other penguins waddling on the beach,
Then raised his flaps, coughed a cough, and started on his speech.

"My fellow penguins down below, so small upon the shore -
You see these things? Well, they're called wings, and I know what
they're for."
When the penguins raised their flaps he said, "I'll answer questions
after."
So the penguins all put down their wings and fought against their
laughter.

"The other day I saw a creature just like you and me -
Black and white, a funny walk and bobbing on the sea.
And then, you wouldn't believe it, you see this little guy
Shot straight out of the water and then swam into the sky."

"And here he is, my friends down there,
That creature that swims through the air."

The strange small creature waddled out and walked up to the edge.
He looked down at the penguins and then flew off of the ledge.
The penguins were all bored by now, a puffin nothing new,
And all started to drift away to find something to do.

But the little penguin launched himself and held his wings out wide.
Then flapped them up and down with both self righteousness and
pride.
When he realised a penguin is much bigger than a puffin,
And swam directly downwards, disappearing into nothing.

Only the puffin watched him die,
And whispered, "Penguins cannot fly."

The little penguin rose up past the others on the shore.
He rose up past the puffin who had seen it all before.
He saw a little penguin body floating in the sea.
"I can fly," he thought and flew up high to sit on Jesus' knee.

The whale's teeth

They had to get a helicopter to fly the toothbrush in.
The toothpaste, it arrived by ship, the HMS 'Big Grin'.
The operation at full scale, the last resort they banked on -
To brush the teeth of the great blue whale and help it catch some
                                                          plankton.

The ship was moored beside the whale, the tube facing the bow.
The crane was used to lift the cap - the engineers knew how.
When all was ready, the chopper steady, the rope was gently yanked on-
To lower the brush to the great blue whale and help it catch some
                                                           plankton.

The pilot held it steady as the brush sank to the deck.
It nearly fell into the sea. The crew said, "Flippin' 'eck!"
But, up above, the men held firm, the engine slowly cranked on -
To align the brush with the great blue whale and help it catch some
                                                           plankton.

At the right time the press was closed to squeeze the toothpaste out.
It ran in red and blue and white from that gigantic spout.
The smoke was pouring from the press, but still the engine tanked on -
To squeeze the paste on the great blue whale and help it catch some
                                                           plankton.

They got a bit upon the deck, but that goes without saying.
They forced the whale's mouth open wide, with everybody praying.
The whale's bad breath was worse than death, the ship's oily chains
                                                           clanked on -
To keep the ship stock steady and to help the whale catch plankton.

The brushing took just half an hour, and then the whale's smile shone.
Its breath smelt fine, purely divine, and soon the whale was gone.
It wrote a letter, *'feeling better, there's much you should be thanked on.'*
And now its breath smelt fresh it could creep up and catch some
                                                                    plankton.

Wannabe wildebeest

I want to be on the telly, *said the wildebeest to his mum.*
I don't want to be a nobody - I want to be someone.
Look at the cheetah, so fast and so sleek.
He's being filmed almost every week.
I just want a walk on - I don't want to speak.
I just want to be on TV.

I want to be on the telly. I want to be filmed by the crew.
I want to go down to the water hole, and find something better to do.
Look at the rhino, so slow and serene,
Then charging at cameras and stealing the scene.
I want to get noticed, you know what I mean?
I just want to be on TV.

I want to be on the telly. I want to be feared and revered.
I don't want to be one more beast in the flock, with thick stupid lips and
a beard.
Look at the elephants, all in a line.
Their chance of fame is far greater than mine.
A voiceover bit part would do me just fine.
I just want to be on TV.

I want to be on the telly. There's nothing much more I can say.
I don't want to hide. I'm not happy inside. I can't keep on living this
way.
Look at the lion, star of the show,
Stalking towards me. I've nowhere to go.
I've finally found that supporting role.
Look, Mum, I'm on TV.

Don't get down

Don't bury your head like an ostrich.
Don't get down like a duck.
Don't hang around like a bat underground
Or, like limpets, you're going to get stuck.

Harry and the Hoover

Harry hates the Hoover.
He thinks it's going to get him.
He says his friend had one the same,
And that the Hoover ate him.

Harry hears the Hoover.
Its roar is getting closer.
He looks around and slinks away
To hide behind the sofa.

Harry sees the Hoover.
It's driving up and down.
His eyes are wild, his fur is up.
He doesn't make a sound.

Harry bites the Hoover.
He jumps up and attacks it.
He howls at it and claws at it,
Swipes at it and whacks it.

Harry's in the Hoover,
Just like his friend before him.
So, if your friend spins you a yarn,
Believe him, don't ignore him.

Wannabe wallaby

I want to be a kangaroo,
But I'm only a wallaby.
I want to hop and never stop.
I'm just a wannabe.

He jumps high and I stay low.
Where he goes I want to go.
Everyone knows a kangaroo,
But nobody knows me.

A wild birthday

There was a knock at the door on young Milly's tenth Birthday,
At twenty five minutes to nine.
As she opened it slowly a lady said lowly,
"Sweetheart, could you sign on the line?"

Milly (ten) signed and the lady said, "Darling,
These presents are so hard to shift."
Then, stepping aside, Milly's eyes opened wide
As she took in her unusual gift.

Milly's mother and father were sleeping in late.
They were lazy in every way.
They heard the door close, but continued to doze
As their daughter approached where they lay.

They moaned at their daughter as Milly stood there,
Then reluctantly sat up in bed.
Milly looked sort of sheepish, whilst they looked asleepish.
She took a deep breath, then she said,

"Thanks for my present - it's just what I wanted.
In fact it's a little bit more.
When I asked to adopt a Siberian tiger,
I didn't mean straight to the door.

I felt a certificate or fluffy toy
Would suffice for the money you spent.
But I find it quite funny, and value for money,
That an actual tiger was sent."

Her mother and father just looked at young Milly,
Surprised and a little upset.
They'd not ticked the option for tiger adoption.
How stupid could their daughter get!

And then the door opened, and Milly stepped forward.
And with her, they couldn't believe,
A man eating beast from a land in the East
With a collar on which it said, 'Steve'.

Then Steve the Siberian tiger ran forward
And bounded up on to the bed.
Milly's father and mother ducked under the covers,
Convinced that they soon would be dead.

They both held their breath and awaited sure death
As the seconds and minutes rolled on.
And then Milly's scared Dad said, "I'd be awfully glad
If you get out and check where he's gone."

But his wife said, "No fear! Though I hold you most dear,
You're a man, I'm a woman, so frail.
Go check for yourself if you value your health.
How can tigers be sent in the mail?"

So, with shakes and with shudders, they lowered the covers
To find out just what was occurring.
And their eyes opened wider to see the rare tiger
Asleep on the duvet and purring.

But where was young Milly, whose birthday it was?
The poor girl was nowhere to be seen.
So her mother screamed, "Dash! I've arranged a big bash.
And I've bought chocolate cake and ice-cream!"

Her father cried, "Milly, this joke is so silly!
Oh, Milly dear, please raise your head.
It's Saturday morning, a new day is dawning.
Who'll bring us our coffee in bed?"

Then Steve the Siberian tiger woke up.
He couldn't believe his striped ears.
How selfish! He thought, *Let a lesson be taught.*
And he gobbled up Milly's old dears.

Now Milly and Steve live alone in the house
(That tiger would not eat a child).
They had a great party, and ate good and hearty,
With all of Steve's friends from the wild.

Beetle juice

A spider in cider is my favourite drink,
But a bee in my tea is much better, I think.
A fly in a pie would just go down a treat,
But a moth in a frothy broth cannot be beat.
A slug in a jug with some juice from a bug.
And a cricket? Just lick it, then give it a tug.
Small beasts are so tasty, now wouldn't you say?
Much better than chocolate in every way.

The monkey in my class

I went to school today and found a monkey in my class.
He was sitting on the teacher's desk and chewing on some grass.
Then he hopped across to Samuel's chair and picked a flea out of his
                                                                    hair.
And then he hopped right back and threw the crayons in the air.

He snatched up Christian's packed lunch box and stole all of his food,
Then turned and poked his bum out, which I thought to be quite rude.
He blew a raspberry, grinned like only cheeky monkeys do,
And said, "Quiet class, now settle down. We've lots of work to do!"

Get out of the mud

"Get out of the mud," said the worm to the pig,
"There isn't enough, and you're far too big.
I'm trying to eat it and pass it on through.
I don't want it dripping off you."

"Get out of the mud," said the pig to the worm.
"You've had long enough, now it's surely my turn.
I need to jump in and start rolling about.
It's time that you wriggled on out."

"Get out of the mud," said the hippo aloud.
"They say two is company, three is a crowd.
I'm coming on in, I'm afraid that is that."
And he jumped in and squashed them both flat.

A fine balance

The flea was on the tightrope on the night the big top fell.
He was half way across
The dental floss
And all was going well.
The audience of hundreds clenched their teeth and held their breath,
And watched as the flea,
So skilfully,
Attempted to cheat death.

Then a mote of dust from way up high came floating to the ground.
The audience gasped,
And suddenly grasped
Just what was going down.
But the flea remained oblivious to the danger he was in.
With his arms akimbo,
He remained in limbo,
Balanced on the string.

"Look out," a man in the second row said, but far too quiet to hear.
"We cannot watch!" some children cried, "Mum, why d'you bring us
here?"
And the ringmaster looked on in horror, and cried into his hat.
The strongman cuddled the bearded lady, who cuddled him right back.
The clowns all took their wigs off and then painted on some frowns.
The performing sea lion forgot to breathe and very nearly drowned.
The elephants balanced on top of each other to get a better view.
And the escapologist got all tied up deciding what to do.
The band kept with the drum roll, so they didn't miss a beat.
But the fire eater dropped his fire and set light to his feet.
The magician disappeared into his magic box of tricks.
The lion jumped onto his tamer, knocking him for six.

The horses threw their riders and attempted to break free.
And the human cannonball climbed inside, afraid of what might be.
The Kazinskys sat on the edge of their seats way up on the trapeze.
But no-one feared the impending doom like the acrobatic fleas.

And then it hit. That little bit
Came floating through the cage,
And landed on that fearless flee
Performing on the stage.

The flea he wobbled left, then right.
He almost made it, brave young mite.
But, alas, the rope was far too tight,
And so the flea went down.

He bounced upon the safety net and flew out of the cage.
He landed on the lion, and the wild beast roared in rage.
The lion bit his tamer's hand.
The tamer tried but could not stand
The pain it caused, and ran to get a bandage from backstage.

As he fled past the ringmaster he knocked him out the way,
And crushed his hat. The ringmaster turned red in pure dismay.
Then shouted out, "You stupid fool!"
And scared the seal within its pool,
Who broke the sea lion's only rule and threw his ball away.

It bounced across the ring and crashed into the magic box.
The magician stumbled out and suffered several nasty knocks.
He rolled up to the water tank,
In which the escapologist sank,
And tipped the whole thing over, breaking each and every lock.

The water raged across the stage and soaked all of the clowns.
It shrunk all of their outfits and then washed off all their frowns.
And one of them, an old bank robber,
Was recognised without his clobber,
By half the band who dropped their brass and chased him round and
                                                                round.

The sound of trumpets falling and of drums all going thump
Turn elephants stir crazy, and the top one tried to jump.
First they bobbled, then they wobbled,
And finally the whole stack toppled,
Spilling jumbos downwards into one great jumbo lump.

They fell upon the strongman's foot who howled into the air,
And threw the bearded lady upwards, pulling out her hair.
The now bald lady gave a cry,
And barely flew into the sky,
And hit the main Kazinsky guy, sat high up on his chair.

The great Kazinsky fell just like the elephants had before,
Screaming like a banshee from the high wire to the floor.
He landed on a cowering horse,
But facing back to front, of course.
The stallion bucked with so much force and headed for the door.

The fire eater stood there in the centre of it all.
He'd remained unharmed, slightly alarmed, when he saw the elephants
                                                                fall.
He kicked off both his smouldering shoes,
Which landed on a nearby fuse,
Which wasn't very welcome news for the human cannonball.

As a silence fell over the circus,
The ringmaster rose to his feet.
He grabbed hold the hand
Of both wild beast and man,
And then bowed to the crowd in their seats.

But, before the first hands started clapping,
A small boy in the front row said, "Hush!"
And everyone heard
A slight sound like a bird
Rustling nervously 'round in a bush.

Then the smell of the sulphur took over,
And the man in the cannon cried, "No!"
But already loaded,
The cannon exploded
And signalled the end of the show.

The audience stood and applauded
As the big top collapsed to the ground.
And on top of the pole,
With a final drum roll,
Bowed the flea to a rapturous sound.

A small amphibian

There's a lizard like creature that lives in my pond.
He's a little bit scary, but cute.
He's slippery and slimy, and ever so tiny.
In fact you could say he's my newt.

Not an otter

I am not an otter -
I'm a beaver, through and through.
It's a common misconception
Between other otters who
Are not a beaver either -
They are otters to the core.
But I am not an otter,
I shall emphasize once more.

Crazy hedgehog

Tarantulas don't scare me,
And scorpions beware me,
'Cause I'm a crazy hedgehog
Who eats bugs and grubs for tea.

There's nothing much that scares me
Except, perhaps, for Mary,
'Cause she's a crazy monster
Who eats hedgehogs just like me.

Judge Gerbil and the rat

Judge gerbil was a mean, old judge.
He kept a rigid court.
He'd stop his wheel and give a squeal
Whenever the accused was brought.

One day whilst riding round and round,
He quashed his revolution,
And called the jury to wake up.
'Twas time for retribution.

The hamsters brought the suspect in
To plead before the judge.
And in his eyes, without disguise,
There lived a vengeful grudge.

"Your honour," spoke one hamster guard,
"This mean looking old rat
Was caught trying to eat your mum.
Sir, what d'you make of that?"

"Eat my mum?" Judge Gerbil cried,
"Of all the bloomin' cheek."
"She tastes like bread," the old rat said,
"That's gone off by a week."

"You rotten soul, you dirty rat!
(Please scratch that last cliché).
My poor, old mum. What had she done?
I'm going to make you pay!"

"Your honour, I plead innocence!"
"Then, let me hear your plea."
"I never swallowed your old mum,
Just dunked her in my tea."

"Oh, no!" Judge Gerbil cried in pain.
"You drowned her. That's so bad."
"But she was trying to interrupt
My nibbling on your dad."

The judge was back upon the wheel,
Rotating, full of tears.
He'd never heard such an excuse
In all his judging years.

"You monster! Have you no remorse?"
The courtroom gasped in shock.
"I sentence you to death by plague.
Now, take him from the dock!"

But that old rat just couldn't resist,
And said, "My tummy hurts.
I wish I hadn't eaten
Your wife and children for desserts."

'Young' Poems

These poems are for people young,
For people old to read,
While people stupid sit and pick their noses.
Then people old can go downstairs
To see the people stupid,
While people young all shut their eyes and dozes.

Mike Lucas

Down in the woods where the bears go, "Boo!"

Down in the woods where the bears go, "Boo!"
I went in search of the Golden Blue.
Twelve feet wide with its wings unfurled,
The rarest of birds in the whole wide world.
Golden feathers and eyes of blue,
Down in the woods where the bears go, "Boo!"

Down in the woods where the bears go, "Boo!"
I went in search of the Golden Blue.
I looked under bushes and up in the trees,
High on my tippy toes and low on my knees.
There wasn't anything that I wouldn't do,
Down in the woods where the bears go, "Boo!"

Down in the woods where the bears go, "Boo!"
I went in search of the Golden Blue.
I heard a strange noise and I stood stock still.
I gazed down the valley and I looked up the hill.
Over the forest a great bird flew,
Down in the woods where the bears go, "Boo!"

Down in the woods where the bears go, "Boo!"
I went in search of the Golden Blue.
I followed the bird to the darkest bush,
Nothing there moved and the woods went, *'hush.'*
I pulled back a branch as a cold wind blew,
And out from the bush a bear went, "Boo!"

Countdown

10, and I am ready. I'm going to the moon.
9, and engines started. I'll be away quite soon.
8, I press the buttons that will help me fly away.
7, and I check the dials - everything's okay.
6, I hear the rumbling getting louder in my ears.
5, I feel some movement and then everybody cheers.
4, I'm a bit nervous now. Have I got everything?
3, I'm sure there's something else that I forgot to bring.
2, the flames shoot upwards as my rocket starts to rise.
1, I see the people and they look as small as flies.
Lift off....and I realise the thing that I forgot.
My teddy's in my bedroom so I'm going to have to STOP!

My wish for vegetables

I'd like to find a vegetable that everyone would eat:
That wasn't green, but red and blue instead.
If it tasted of ice-cream, then it would surely be a treat,
Instead of something in my dinner that I dread.

What makes the waves?

My science teacher asked of me,
"What is the cause of the waves in the sea?
Why does the ocean rise and fall?
Do you know at all?"

I scratched my head and I said to he,
"Is it the ships that sail the sea?
Or the southerly wind? Or the rains that pour?
I'm really not that sure.

Is it the monsters that lurk beneath,
When they swish their tails and they gnash their teeth?
Or the warm volcanoes that erupt below?
Please tell me, I don't know.

Is it the continents drifting around?
Or the oil that they drill from underground?
Or pirates of old from beyond the grave?
So what's the cause of the waves?"

He said, "I'll tell you - it's none of these
That makes the waves on the Seven Seas.
It isn't the ships or the winds that blow.
It isn't the rain or the monsters below.
It isn't volcanoes or lands on the drift,
Or buccaneers with immortality's gift.

But look at the sky from your window tonight,
And the man in the moon with his silvery light.
And the way that he moves 'cross the southern sky.
Then you'll know the reason why."

Smelly toes

If five and five is ten, and ten and ten is twenty,
That's the sum of all my fingers and my toes.
And, because my hands are dirty and my feet are always smelly,
It's a good job that I only have one nose.

A strange tribe

Whilst down in the woodland I found a new race
Who wore colourful clothes and put paint on their face.
They talked a strange language and had a strange smell.
Were they happy or angry? I just couldn't tell.
They had hair down their backs and their claws, they were long.
They spoke in high voices and sometimes in song.
They took it in turns to perform a weird dance
Which I watched from my hideout, enthralled and entranced.
I forgot to stay hidden. They heard me I think.
They chased me and caught me and dressed me in pink.
They blushed up my cheeks, tied my hair up in curls,
And said, "That'll teach you for spying on girls!"

Dizzy below

If the Earth spins around as it travels through space,
And Australia lies on the southern face,
When I visit Aunt Sheila and Great Uncle Ted,
Will I get dizzy and fall out of bed?

Where to go today?

I've often thought of travelling up to the moon and back,
But I haven't got a rocket for the ride.
I wouldn't get too far, perhaps a foot into the air,
So I suppose I'm going to have to stay inside.

I've often thought of going to the bottom of the sea,
But I need a submarine to take me down.
I've only got a snorkel and a mask and that's no good,
So I suppose I'm going to have to stick around.

I've often thought of dragon hunting back in days of old,
But I haven't got my armour or a sword.
I've got a hobby horse, but it doesn't go too fast,
So I suppose I'm going to have to stay indoors.

I've often thought of being a fearless pirate on the waves,
But I haven't got a pirate ship or crew.
I've got a rubber ring, but it isn't quite the same,
So I suppose my bedroom's going to have to do.

I've been a racing driver and a cowboy with a gun.
I've been an engineer just like my dad.
I've been a famous footballer and that one was quite fun.
But being me is the mostest fun I ever had.

Pick a favourite

What's your favourite nettle in a field of nettle plants?
In a drawer of all your underwear, what are your favourite pants?
What's your favourite grain of sand upon a sandy beach?
And, in a peachy punnet, what's the punnet's perfect peach?
What's your favourite word within a dictionary of words?
And, in a flock of flying fish, which fish is your preferred?
What's your favourite star of all the stars that you can see?
And, out of all the me's you know, which one's your favourite me?

I'm not tired

Why can't I stay up and watch TV?
My sister's asleep but she's not me.
She's little three, but I'm big four.
Please, ten minutes more?

Why can't I stay up and play my game?
My dad's asleep and snoring again.
He's so old, but I'm still young.
Five more minutes, mum?

Why can't I stay up to finish my cup?
I'm talking mum, so please wake up.
You're head's all droopy, but mine's okay.
Two more minutes to play!

I've finished my drink and I'm tired, dear Ted.
But no-one's awake to take me to bed.
I need tucking in and a kiss goodnight,
And someone to leave on the landing light.
Please lay down beside me and don't make a peep.
I need to go to sleep.

What's the sense of weather?

You can't hear lightning, you can't see thunder.
Why can't you do those things? I wonder.

You can't touch rainbows, you can't smell snow.
Why that is, I just don't know.

You can't taste wind or speak to rain.
Why is that? I ask again.

And when you put these facts together,
You find there's just no sense to weather.

How high is the sky?

How high is the sky? Is it all the way and back?
Does it go from here to there or further still?
Is it longer than forever? Is it mostly blue or black?
I do not know and s'pose I never will.

How deep is the sea? From the bottom to the top?
Is it as far as you can go or even more?
Does it end before you get there? If I sink when will I stop?
If there's an answer I will never know for sure.

How long is the world going to keep on spinning round?
Will it stop awhile, then spin the other way?
If it stopped all of a sudden would my feet float off the ground?
They may not do this, but then again they may.

How far would I go for you? Is there a limit to my love?
To keep you safe what is the price I'd pay?
To this I know the answer, for it's written up above.
Everything and more is what I'd say.

My penny

Where was my penny yesterday?
Was it near of far away?
What was it spent on?
Who did the spending?
Was it lent out?
Who did the lending?
Maybe a pirate had buried it once.
Maybe a referee tossed it.
But now it is mine 'cause I found it today.
And if it was yours then you've lost it.

Little Johnny (a cautionary tale for children)

Little Johnny at the tea table was not a pretty sight,
For he didn't like to eat what had been brought.
He would play with it and mash it and then push it 'round his plate.
No, he didn't behave the way he should've ought.

If his mother cooked potatoes he would say, "I want some chips!"
And with chips he'd say, "I don't like them like that!"
And then after she had changed them and said, "Sorry, Johnny dear."
He wouldn't eat them but would sneak them to the cat.

Now, one day when all the family had baked beans and mash for tea
And our Johnny did his usual little trick,
His mother said, "I'm sorry, but please try to eat it, Johnny."
Well, his tummy made a noise and he was sick.

So, the doctor, he was called out and he brought his bag of stuff -
A tape measure and some medicine that was red.
The colour of the medicine wasn't right for little Johnny,
So the doctor went and measured him instead.

This frightened Johnny's mother, but the doctor said, "Don't worry,
I'm not measuring for the reason that you think.
But from everything you've told me, and from studying my notes,
I'm concerned that Johnny may begin to shrink."

But, still Johnny didn't eat right for a week or maybe more.
He was fussy, he was naughty, he was bad.
Whatever dish was put upon the table by his mother,
He just pushed it 'round his plate, the silly lad.

So the doctor came once more to test his theory on the boy,
Took his measure out and measured him again.
Then he turned around to mother and said, "Well, that proves my case.
He has gone from three foot two to two foot ten."

Well, his mother shouted, "No! What can I do to make him eat?
Tell me, Johnny dear, what would you like for tea?"
But Johnny said, "Come mother, stop the bluffing, he's no doctor -
Yes, I know you're trying to play a trick on me."

And the days they came and went, but Johnny carried on the same,
Till one day he went to climb upon his bed.
But his legs, they wouldn't lift, he couldn't make it up the step,
So he had to sleep down on the floor instead.

When he woke he felt all funny as he stood and stretched himself.
Then he looked around his room and had a shock.
For his bedroom had grown bigger, as had all the stuff inside,
And at night he must have climbed inside a sock.

Now, that feeling in his tummy became stronger all the time,
And he trembled as he headed for the door.
But he couldn't reach the handle, which had moved up way too high,
So he fell into a heap upon the floor.

When his mother shouted, "Johnny, I've put cereal on the table!"
Little Johnny's tummy rumbled with delight.
For he thought, *I won't be fussy any longer, that I promise,*
If it means that I will get me back some height.

But instead he kept on shrinking, now no bigger than a fly,
Now a flea and very soon not even that.
And as he squeezed under the door a breeze came by and swept him up
And, floating freely, he was breathed in by the cat.

Well, his mother never found him, though she still looks high and low,
And Little Johnny isn't Johnny any more.
For he shrank away to nothing and remains that way today,
Though exactly where he is I can't be sure.

And the moral of the story is (for boys and girls alike)
When your mother brings your tea then do what's right.
Do not push it 'round your plate, but sit and eat it like you should,
Or you'll disappear like Johnny overnight!

Big eared baldy baby

I saw a big eared baldy baby
Lying in a pram.
The big eared baldy baby said,
"Do you know who I am?"
I told him I was sorry,
But I didn't recognise
His pretty little button nose
Or cute baby blue eyes.

Do you know where the Bobblebears go?

Do you know where the Bobblebears go
When the Googleray comes to town?
Because I don't know where the Bobblebears go,
But I know that they don't hang around.

Do they go to the Carroty Wood?
Or the Hills of Click (I think they should)?
Do they trek across the Desert of Cree?
Or swim across the Spandipan Sea?

Maybe they wade across the River of Sneer,
Or the Swamps of Ponk (that's the best idea).
Maybe they fly to the Clouds of Squore,
Or flee to the Dampy Moor.

I bet they run to the Icy Strew,
Or the Lakes of Jerb (that's what I'd do).
Or perhaps they sink to the bottom of the Schpoon,
Or float to the Wilvery Moon.

Tonight I went where the Bobblebears go
When the Googleray comes to town.
I followed them through the Carroty Wood
To the Hills of Click (like I said they should).
Then they headed across the Desert of Cree,
And swam across the Spandipan Sea.
They waded across the River of Sneer
To the Swamps of Ponk (my favourite idea).

I followed them up to the Clouds of Squore
And down to the Dampy Moor.
We ran and skated to the Icy Strew,
Past the Lakes of Jerb (like I knew they'd do).
And after we sank to the bottom of the Schpoon,
We floated to the Wilvery Moon.

But still they travelled and I followed behind,
Tired and weary and wondering what I'd find,
Till they stopped in a land unknown to me,
Where I saw a sign on an Oojaloop tree,
Which read, *'To our guests from far away,*
Welcome to the land of the Googleray'.

Little boy, fluffy toy

Little boy
Fluffy toy
In his bed
Sleepy head
Lullabies
Close his eyes
Dreaming deep
Not a peep

Another day
Out to play
Friends to meet
In the street
Playing rough
Acting tough
Girls outside
Run and hide

Fluffy toy
Waits for boy

The rocking horse

My rocking horse no longer rocks.
My dad has had it up on blocks.
He's going to oil and grease it
And he's going to test the shocks.

He'll rub it down and paint it
And he'll make a seat on which to sit.
He'll tighten all the nuts,
And then the rocking horse will rock.

It's strange because I don't recall
Having a rocking horse at all.
I've asked my dad if I can see,
But he says, "Go and play."

So I'm going to walk my dog with friends
Until my rocking horse, he mends.
I've called him but, that ragged mutt
Has not been seen all day.

Now here's my dad, he's looking pleased.
"It rocks," he says, "It's oiled and greased.
I've tightened up the nuts
And made a seat for it, of course."

And behind him, on a piece of string,
The rocking horse is following.
"As good as new," murmurs my dad.
"Woof," says my new horse.

My fateful wish

I threw a penny down a well to conjure up some luck.
It bounced off of the brickwork and it killed a passing duck.
I threw another penny in so I could make a wish.
It completely knocked the brickwork off and killed all of the fish.
I've only got one penny left, the fish and duck are dead.
So I think I'll keep this penny and depend on fate instead.

Mum! Mum! Mum!

Mum, can I go out to play?
I know it's raining but that's okay.
I've got my coat and my wellies too.
I won't come in to use the loo.
Mum, I'm bored. Can I go out
And see who is about?

Mum, can we come in to play?
I know it's sunny, but that's okay.
There's three of us, we'll wipe our feet,
Play in my room and keep it neat.
Mum, we're bored, can we come in
Until it rains again?

'Language' Poems

These poems are called 'Language'.
They're about the way we speak,
Or maybe read and write like what we do.
I've written them in English,
Which is easier than Greek,
Though some of them may seem like Greek to you.

No poems are coming tonight

No poems are coming tonight.
My eyelids are drooping,
I'm losing my sight.
I can't find a thought
Or a word that is right.
I think that I'll call it a night.

No poems are coming tonight.
My head keeps on nodding,
There's nothing to write.
But I'm writing down nothing
Till dawn's early light.
I wish I could call it a night.

No poems are coming tonight.
I wish you'd stop reading -
It's only polite -
Because when you stop reading
This poem I might
Be able to call it a night.

Gobbledegook

If me speaks all like dis when me is only free or four,
Den all de peoples dat me meets finks me is coot.
But if me speaks all like dis when me is nearly firty five
Den dey's gonna fink dat me is loopy loop.

Breaking the rule

I cannot stop the rhymes.
They keep on coming all the time.
Whoops! You see, there goes another one.
Every line you see
Has to rhyme so perfectly.
Except for this last line, which doesn't.

The colour of my poem

Carrots are orange, and oranges too.
The sunshine is golden, the wild wind's blue.
Violets are violet and Black is the Sea.
But red is the poem that's written by me.

Useless poem

Got to keep writing,
Got to fill a book.
Got to pen another one,
No matter how it look.

Got to get a line out,
Second line should rhyme.
People will read anything
If it kills the time.

A book will make me famous,
A book will make me rich.
I've got to build a platform
From which to make a pitch.

Maybe this one's rubbish,
A poem for poem's sake.
But I bet you've read from start to end,
And I bet you're still awake.

How (not) to write a limerick

A limerick's very first line
Should rhyme with the next every time.
The fourth's final word
Should rhyme with the third.
But I can never get the last one quite right.

Writer's block

I was writing a poem about an old sock,
But then I got writer's block…

M.N.E.M.O.N.I.C.

A mnemonic is a group of words that helps you to remember
Other groups of words like January to December.
It rings a bell, is hard to spell, but see below for ease:
Many Nervous Elephants Mix Orange Nuts In Cheese.

The motivation behind a poem

Because I want to write a poem
About a stupid skunk,
I need another rhyming word,
And so that skunk gets drunk.

And because the poem's far too short
To make it worth my while,
I give that skunk a scary friend -
A hungry crocodile.

And because I want to finish now
And sneak off up to bed,
The crocodile can eat the skunk
And suddenly drop dead.

A body of grammar

I often juxtapose
My finger with my nose,
Hyperbolise
My big fat gut with mouth watering pies.
My heart is filled with bathos -
It beats in time to what I say.
And my brain is just a metaphor
For why I write this way.

A very different poem

I've never penned a poem which is like this one right now,
'Cause this one's totally different from the rest.
It's the only one where I have written vest eleven times -
Vest, vest, vest, vest, vest, vest, vest, vest, vest.

The same as opposite

The opposite of opposite
Is something that's the same.
An antonym's the same as opposite.
And if you want the same as same
A synonym will do.
So don't be fooled,
That's all there is to it.

Somefink

I don't know nuffink
About nuffink,
I don't fink.
But somefink
That I fink
Is that you stink.

Eether or neether?

Is it ither or eether?
Or nither or neether?
Is ither one right or is neether?
When I'm in conversation,
Which pronunciation?
I'm nearing the end of my teether (or tither).

Granama

An granama is a proug of slerett
That, rearranged, makes misethong berett.
It soten'd have to make chum snees,
Necnocted by a bustle phreas.

Hoity-toity poem

I'm going to write a poem
That doesn't rhyme.
It doesn't mean I'm a failure,
Or one of those hoity-toities
Who just takes words:
Perhaps short, rarely used epigrams,
And strings them together in irregular rhythmic patterns
That make it difficult to
Read
In context, or interpret (translate).
Yes, that's what I'm going to do.
I'm going to write a poem that doesn't rhyme.
But just this one time.
Drat!

'My' Poems

These poems are about me.
Their subject is myself.
They're all about dimensions of my life.
I mention all my cats a lot,
My children and my gran.
And somewhere here I talk about my wife.

Mike Lucas

My hair

My hair fell out when I was twenty.
Up till then my head held plenty.
It came back after twenty years,
From down my nose and out my ears.

My family (when I'm away)

I know a little girl who loves her mermaids.
She collects them and she has one on her wall.
I know a little boy who likes all kinds of superheroes.
He fights like them when playing in the hall.

I know a girl who likes her mathematics,
Adding up the numbers in her head.
And I know a boy who likes to run around and make some noise,
Though sometimes I wish he'd sit and read instead.

I know a little girl who likes to colour.
She likes arts and crafts and doing it herself.
I know a little boy who still adores his cuddly toys.
He has lots of them arranged upon his shelf.

I know a little boy who is five (but nearly six),
And a little girl who's seven (but nearly eight).
And their mummy's thirty one (although she's nearly thirty two).
And I'll soon be with them all - I just can't wait.

My gran

I went to see my gran today.
She lives in a home not far away.
She asked me who I was, and then
She asked me who I was again.

My cats (when they lived in Switzerland)

There once were three cats called Tigger, Sam and Ellie
Who learnt to speak French from the news on the telly.
"Une bière, s'il vous plait," would be Sam's favourite phrase,
As he sat at the restaurant on sunny days.
He would look at the girls and would cat-whistle at them.
And they would say, "Ooh-la-la, mais Monsieur vous êtes 'andsome."
Then Sam would say, "Oui, mais'ow can you resist?
Viens ici maintenant, give us a kiss."

Now Ellie was pretty and black like the night.
She loved to chase mice and would kill with delight.
She favoured the wines when she rabbit fondued,
And did not fancy Sam, who she thought was too crude.
"I 'ave never liked men, I prefer them afar.
Now drink up your bière and dît-moi au revoir."
But Sam would just sit there and think her absurd.
And then he'd drink up and go find him a bird.

Well, Tigger was different, but how I'm not sure.
He loved to just lay there, but preferred a soft floor.
His habit was dirty, you know what I mean?
He wasn't exactly the cleanest of clean.
But he gave lots of cuddles, and he had a good heart.
Though during the cuddle sometimes he would fart.
And the French that he learnt? With you that I will share -
"Mais sorry, Madame, I 'ave oui oui'd on your chair."

My bogey box

I have myself a bogey box.
I keep my bogies under locks.
And every time I pick my nose,
In the box it goes.

My hamster

Nobody said that my hamster was dead
When I went out to feed it today.
It didn't even move when I gave it a smooth
Or when I set light to the hay.
I though a cremation a nice celebration
Of a life that was short but so sweet.
But I hadn't been told, in the winter so cold,
That a hamster enjoys a long sleep.

My cat, Max

I've got a three legged cat called Max.
He's got two front but only one backs.
He still runs fast when I put him out the house.
Then he sits there waiting for a three legged mouse.

My Christmas birthday

I want a Christmas party, but I want it for my birthday
In July, with all my friends around for tea.
We're going to sing some carols like, '*God bless you merry birthday*
                                                                        presents,'
And put a birthday cake below the tree.

We may well play a game like pass the parcel, but with crackers,
And then pin the tail on donkey in a manger with some hay.
We'll have turkey with some candles, and then walk around in sandals,
Just like Mary and like Joseph did on Jesus' first birthday.

My Great Uncle Tommy

My Great Uncle Tommy lost a leg in the war
And nobody handed it in.
Lost Property said, "Leave your details with us,
And we'll check every now and again."

Now, sixty years later, his leg has turned up
In a box at the back of the store.
We're so grateful the leg is alive and back home.
But Great Uncle Tom is no more.

My disgusting habit

When there's nothing on TV
I pick my toe nails aimlessly.
And once I've got a nice, sharp bit,
I pick my teeth with it.

My visitor

I awoke late last night to the pale moonlight
And a scritch and a scratch in my room.
I lifted my head and I climbed out of bed
And I fumbled about in the gloom.

I rubbed at my eyes and I yawned, oh so wide
As a scritch and a scratch scurried past.
And then consciousness came, as it whispered my name
And awoke me with fear unsurpassed.

It said:

"I used to live here in the room at the top,
A long time before this house was built.
And if you heed me well, and this tale that I tell,
You will learn from your ancestors' guilt.

Over one hundred years before you and your kind
Came and lived on this land with your folk,
There were acres of forest, of sycamores, elms,
And to rule overall, a great oak.

And my family lived here, many others like me,
And many more different, in peace.
In the sycamore, elm and the mighty great oak
Dwelt every conceivable beast.

But the monsters then came, with their weapons and noise,
And destroyed all the things we held dear.
They cut down the trees, brought the beasts to their knees,
And then drove off the rest in such fear.

My family died and, like them, so did I
As they cut down the mighty great oak.
For three hundred years it had grown from the ground
And, in less than a day, turned to smoke.

I used to live here in this room at the top,
And long before you and your kind.
Your foundations are built on the roots of the oak
And your roof where the ivy entwined.
Your walls are the bark of the king of the forest,
Your windows where owls watched the world.
Your door is the entrance to burrows and tunnels,
And the bricks are where leaves once unfurled.
Your eaves are where towers of branches spread forth,
Your chimney where birds built there nests.
The tiles are the scars of the storms that bore down,
But your room is the place where I rest.

I used to live here in this room at the top,
Then my short life was taken away.
Your bed was my bed at the top of the tree,
Where I dwelt with my kin in my drey.

But have you your house on your land in the town
Where the trees of the forest once stood.
Though the oak is no more, its great spirit remains
As the king of the heavenly wood."

Then the squirrel fell quiet and I heard from my room
A scritch and a scratch once again.
And I followed the noise to the eaves in the roof
And I heard from outside the wild rain.

Then, cowering down to the door in the side,
I opened it slowly to find
The branches and leaves of a drey in my eaves
With a family of squirrels inside.

Then the scritch and the scratch of their ancestor's ghost
Floated up to the roof and away.
And I closed the small door
And then dwelt there some more
On the squirrels who lived in the drey.

My bath

Some people say that baths are more relaxing,
Therapeutic and so good for your well-being.
But I say that a shower is far more invigorating,
And certainly more hygienic to wee in.

My little toe

I do not like my little toe.
It goes not where my others go.
When my toes are all in bed
My little toe goes out instead.
I asked my toe to stop and linger,
But it ran off with my small finger.

My broken radio

There's a radio upon a shelf at home that doesn't work.
It plays a lot of nothing all the time.
I can turn the volume up and hear a peace playing so clearly,
And listen to a live performing mime.

I can tune it into perfect hush or maybe soundless singing,
And hum along without making a sound.
It's even got a mute button in case it gets too much,
And the deafening silence needs to be turned down.

My luvvy duvvy poem

There's never been a hedgehog on the moon.
There's never been a knife and fork who've wrestled with a spoon.
There's never been an orange with a pair of arms or legs,
Or an elephant that flies hot air balloons.

There's never been a poem without words.
There's never been a bottle bank for stamp collecting birds.
There's never been a rhubarb stalk that's passed a driving test,
And to think of singing pencils is absurd.

There's never been a moment since I met you
When I think of other things and then forget you.
There's never been a person in this strange revolving world
Who has loved another person more, I bet you.

My epitaph

On my gravestone it must say
Here lies Mike, who rhymed all day.
He had so many in his head,
He's even rhyming when he's dead.